W9-AVA-285

Comets, Asteroids, and Meteors

Dr. Raman K. Prinja

Heinemann Library
Chicago, Illinois

© 2003 Reed Educational & Professional Publishing
Published by Heinemann Library,
an imprint of Reed Educational & Professional Publishing,
Chicago, Illinois

Customer Service 888-454-2279

Visit our website at www.heinemannlibrary.com

Designed Jo Hinton-Malivoire
Page Layout by AMR
Originated by Dot Gradations Ltd.
Printed in Hong Kong, China by Wing King Tong

07 06 05 04 03
10 9 8 7 6 5 4 3 2 1

Library of Congress Cataloging-in-Publication Data
Prinja, Raman, 1961-
    Comets, asteroids, and meteors / Raman Prinja.
        v. cm. -- (The universe)
Includes bibliographical references and index.
Contents: What are comets, asteroids, and meteors? -- Where do comets come from and why do they have tails? -- What is a comet made of? -- Which are the most famous comets? -- Do comets ever crash? -- What is an asteroid? -- Why do we study asteroids? -- What is a meteor shower? -- What is the difference between meteors and meteorites?
    ISBN 1-58810-909-7 (hardcover) -- ISBN 1-40340-610-3 (pbk.)
  1. Comets--Juvenile literature. 2. Asteroids--Juvenile literature.
3. Meteors--Juvenile literature. [1. Comets. 2. Meteors. 3. Asteroids.] I. Title. II. Series.
    QB721.5 .P75 2002
    523.6--dc21
                            2002004058

Acknowledgments
The author and publishers are grateful to the following for permission to reproduce copyright material:
pp. 4, 5, 8, 10, 12, 14, 15, 16, 17, 19, 20, 22, 23, 24, 26, 28, 29/Science Photo Library; pp. 6, 13, 25/NASA; p. 7/Astrophoto; p. 11/AKG London; p.21/Johns Hopkins University (Applied Physics Laboratory); p.27/Galaxy Picture Library.

Cover photograph reproduced with permission of Science Photo Library.

The author would like to thank Kamini, Vikas, Sachin and all his family for their support.

The publisher would like to thank Geza Gyuk and Diana Challis of the Adler Planetarium for their comments in the preparation of this book.

Every effort has been made to contact copyright holders of any material reproduced in this book. Any omissions will be rectified in subsequent printings if notice is given to the publisher.

Some words are shown in **bold,** like this. You can find out what they mean by looking in the glossary.

Contents

What Are Comets, Asteroids, and Meteors?

Billions of lumps of ice and rock called comets and asteroids exist in our **solar system.** When a bit of rock from space enters Earth's **atmosphere,** it heats up and makes a light streak called a meteor. These objects are left over from when the solar system formed about 4.5 billion years ago.

This picture shows Comet Hyakutake, which crossed our skies in March 1996.

This is a close-up view of the head and tail of Comet Hyakutake.

Comets

Comets are like dirty snowballs. They are made of ice, dust, and gases. They travel around the Sun in long oval-shaped **orbits.** As they get closer to the Sun, the ice melts and a gigantic tail of gas and dust forms.

Comets are rarely seen in the sky. Spectacular ones with beautiful long tails appear about once every ten to fifteen years. More often they look like faint, fuzzy "stars." Although comets travel very fast in space, they seem to move slowly across the sky when tracked over several nights because they are so far away.

Asteroids

Asteroids are lumps of rock drifting in space. Some are as small as 3 feet (1 meter) across or even smaller. Others are nearly as large as a third of the size of Earth's Moon. Almost 100,000 asteroids travel around the Sun between the orbits of Mars and Jupiter.

Only a few asteroids are bright enough for us to see in the sky. Even with a good pair of binoculars or a telescope, they are hard to spot. They do not look very exciting. They look like specks of light.

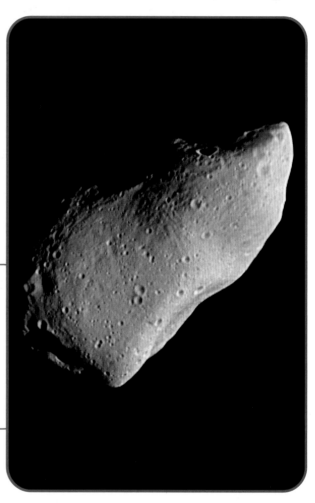

This picture of the asteroid Gaspra was taken by the Galileo *spacecraft when it was only 3,300 miles (5,300 kilometers) away from Gaspra's surface.*

Meteors

Sometimes dust or rocks from space come so close to Earth that **gravity** pulls them into Earth's **atmosphere**. These rocks and dust are called **meteoroids**. Sometimes a meteoroid falls all the way to Earth. A meteoroid that lands on Earth's surface is called a **meteorite**.

This pair of meteors makes a beautiful sight in the sky.

Meteoroids heat up as they plunge through the Earth's atmosphere. The outer layers get stripped away. The fast-moving air around the meteoroid gives off light. These streaks of light are meteors. It takes them just a few seconds to flash across the night sky. That is why meteors are sometimes called "shooting stars" or "falling stars." Meteors can appear in any part of the sky at any time. You can usually see a few every hour. Most meteors look white, but red, yellow, or even green meteor streaks have also been seen.

During some months of the year, many more meteors than usual can be seen. This is a **meteor shower.**

Why Are They Called Comets, Asteroids, and Meteors?

The word "comet" describes a comet's flowing tail, and comes from the ancient Greek word *kometes,* meaning "long-haired."

The ancient Greek word *asteroid* means "like a star."

The word "meteor" comes from the Greek word *meteoron,* which means "a special event in the sky."

Where Do Comets Come From ?

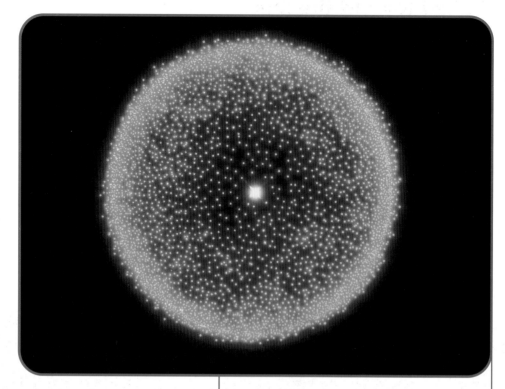

The Oort cloud is home to a huge swarm of comets, which surround the planets in our solar system.

Most of the comets we see in the sky may start their journeys from a very faraway region of our **solar system** called the **Oort cloud.** The Oort cloud is much farther out than the **orbit** of Pluto. Parts of the Oort cloud are 9.3 trillion miles (15 trillion kilometers) away, which is 100,000 times farther away from Earth than the Sun.

There are many billions of comets in the Oort cloud. They are nothing more than very cold lumps of ice, dust, and rock. Most of them are only a few miles across. There are also billions more comets that orbit the Sun. These comets are found between Pluto and the Oort cloud. This second collection of comets is called the **Kuiper belt.**

Pulled toward the Sun

While comets are in the Oort cloud and Kuiper belt, they are frozen, dark objects that we cannot see. They do not glow or have flowing tails. Sometimes, however, a comet can get knocked out of these areas. For example, it might crash into another comet. The comet's path is then changed. The Sun's **gravity** pulls it toward the inner part of the solar system.

Their new orbits around the Sun are not as close to being circles as the orbits of most of the **planets**. Comets travel in a long, oval-shaped orbit. Comets can take hundreds or even thousands of years to complete one journey around the Sun.

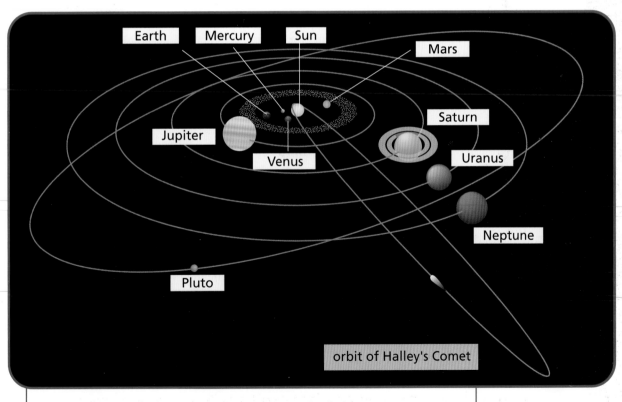

The comets seen in the sky move around the Sun in stretched-out, oval orbits. All the planets except Pluto have almost circular orbits.

Why Do Comets Have Tails?

As a comet gets closer to the Sun, it begins to heat up and glow. What started as a dark, frozen object turns into one so bright that we can see it from Earth. This change happens because the heat from the Sun melts the ice on the comet's surface. The heated gases now reflect the Sun's light and begin to glow. The comet starts to squirt huge fountains of gas and dust into space.

Two tails

As the comet nears the Sun, the jets of gas and dust make huge tails that stretch for millions of miles. As the comet moves closer to the Sun, more than 100,000 pounds (45,360 kilograms) of gas and dust may escape from the comet every second! The comet may now appear as a bright point of light in our skies.

Comets have two types of tails. They have a **dust tail** made of **microscopic** grains of dust. A dust tail is not straight, but is slightly curved. Comets also have a blue **gas tail** made of hot gas, which is straighter and narrower.

The tail of a comet always points away from the Sun. This is because it is being pushed back by a flow of electric **particles** flowing off the Sun. This flow is called the **solar wind.** The solar wind acts like a fan that blows the comet's tail away from the Sun.

Comet West was seen in the skies during March 1976. It had a narrow blue gas tail and a wide white dust tail.

The end of the show

After many months, a comet will move around the Sun and head back into the outermost parts of the **solar system.** As it glides away from the heat of the Sun, the comet's surface cools down and starts to freeze over again. It returns to being a dark object that can no longer be seen from Earth. It may be hundreds or thousands of years before that same comet returns to our part of the solar system and heats up to once again put on a display.

Scary Comets

Comets in the sky have caused fear and panic through the ages. For thousands of years people thought comets brought bad news. This is because, unlike the Sun, Moon, and stars, comets came and went without warning.

Comets have been blamed for many things on Earth. In 79 C.E., a comet appeared in the sky during the eruption of Mount Vesuvius, a volcano that destroyed the Roman city of Pompeii.

Some people, however, thought that comets were a good sign. A comet appeared in 44 B.C.E., soon after the death of the Roman leader Julius Caesar. The comet was said to be a sign that the dead leader had become a god.

The famous Bayeaux Tapestry in France shows Halley's Comet (upper right) in 1066.

What Is a Comet Made Of?

Along with its tail, a comet has two other main parts called a **nucleus** and a **coma**.

*This is how the nucleus of Halley's Comet looked from the Giotto **spacecraft** in 1986.*

Fragile nucleus

The solid part at the center of a comet is the nucleus. It may be only a few miles across. Unlike a **planet,** which is shaped like a ball, a comet has an odd shape. Its nucleus is made of loose dust and rock that is held together by ice. The ice is made of frozen water and also frozen gases such as **carbon dioxide.**

A comet's coma

When a comet gets near the Sun, the ice in the nucleus starts to boil away and gases begin to escape. This is when the nucleus becomes surrounded by a cloud of material called a coma. The bright coma can measure more than 60,000 miles (100,000 kilometers) across. That's nearly the size of the giant planet Saturn. The largest coma ever measured was almost the size of the Sun. The coma and the nucleus together make up the head of the comet.

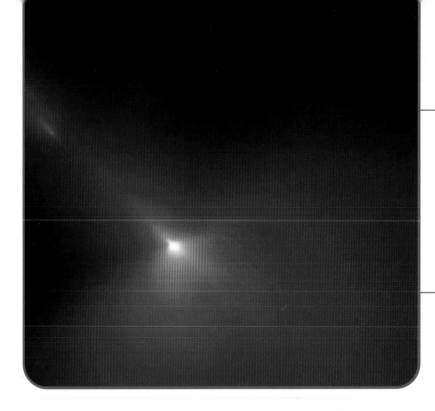

The fuzzy spot in this picture is the growing coma of Comet Hyakutake, seen in March 1996.

Has Anyone Been Really Close to a Comet?

A few spacecraft have flown very close to comets. One of these was the *Giotto* spacecraft, which flew to within 370 miles (600 kilometers) of Halley's Comet in 1986. *Giotto* discovered the comet had an oval-shaped nucleus that was 9.3 miles (15 kilometers) long and 5 miles (8 kilometers) wide. There were hills and valleys on the surface of the comet, with powerful jets of gas streaming out to make a tail.

Another spacecraft, called *Stardust,* was launched in 1999 toward Comet Wild. *Stardust* will collect dust from the comet in 2004 and bring it back to Earth for scientists to study. The material from the comet will teach us new things about what the **solar system** was made of when it formed billions of years ago.

Which Are the Most Famous Comets?

Thousands of comets have been discovered, but only a few of the brightest and most exciting to watch are well-known today.

Halley's Comet

The most famous comet in history is Halley's Comet. It is named after the British **astronomer** Edmond Halley, who first worked out the comet's **orbit** in 1705. Although most comets are named after the people who first find them, Halley did not discover this comet. Chinese astronomers saw it more than 2,000 years ago.

Halley's Comet passes through our skies about every 76 years. It last appeared in 1986 and will return in the year 2062. Along its orbit in 1986, the comet came within 50 million miles (80 million kilometers) of the Sun and passed by the Earth at a distance of about 40 million miles (65 million kilometers).

Sir Edmond Halley (1656–1742) was a famous British astronomer.

Hale-Bopp

Comet Hale-Bopp was a dazzling sight in the night skies during 1997. At the head of the comet was a very bright **coma**, which was followed by two sweeping tails.

Millions of people watched Comet Hale-Bopp in the skies during 1997.

Hale-Bopp passed by Earth at a distance of about 122 million miles (197 million kilometers). That's nearly one and a half times the distance between Earth and the Sun. The comet was moving at a speed of about 1.2 million miles per day (2 million kilometers per day). Sadly, Hale-Bopp takes so long to complete an orbit around the Sun that it won't be back in our skies for another 3,600 years!

Comet Kohoutek

Comet Kohoutek was discovered in March 1973 by the Czech astronomer Lubos Kohoutek. He found it by accident, when it was still a long way from the Sun. This comet caused a lot of excitement. People thought that when the comet got closer to the Sun and heated up, it would be the most fantastic comet to be seen in 100 years.

Although it had a beautiful tail, Comet Kohoutek stayed dim and never lived up to expectations. It won't return to our skies for another 75,000 years.

Do Comets Ever Crash?

The Earth's Moon and the **planet** Mercury have a lot of **craters** on their surfaces. Craters are bowl-shaped holes that were made billions of years ago when comets, asteroids, or **meteorites** hit a planet's or a moon's surface. Some comets pass so close to the Sun that they get dragged in by its strong **gravity** and disappear forever.

If it weren't for the wearing away, or **erosion,** of land by rain and wind, Earth's surface would also have lots of scars from being hit by objects from space. A few scars do still remain today. Barringer Crater, which is more than 4,000 feet (1,200 meters) wide was left by a meteorite that crashed near Winslow, Arizona, about 50,000 years ago.

A crash into Jupiter

In March 1993, **astronomers** discovered a comet called Shoemaker-Levy 9 that had broken into more than 20 pieces, each about six-tenths of a mile (one kilometer) across. The pieces of the comet passed so close to Jupiter, that the giant planet's strong gravity pulled them in.

Barringer Crater is about 600 feet (180 meters) deep and 4,000 feet (1,200 meters) wide. Twenty football fields could fit on the floor of the crater.

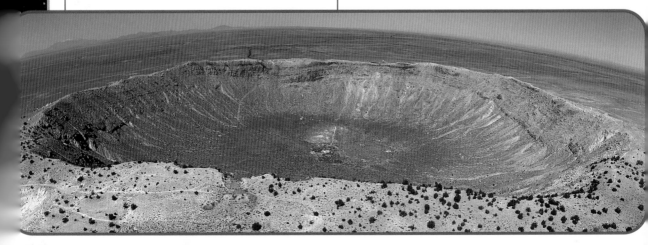

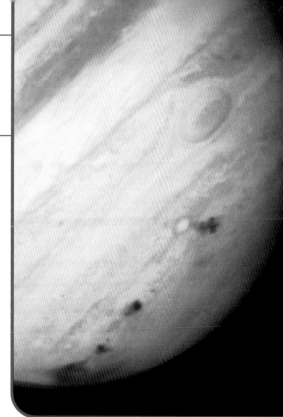

Dark, Earth-sized blotches were seen in the atmosphere of Jupiter after pieces of a comet crashed there.

The broken-up comet finally crashed into Jupiter's **atmosphere** between July 16 and July 22, 1994. The lumps of rock and ice thumped into Jupiter's atmosphere and exploded in huge fireballs. They left large dark blotches made of gas and dust in the upper layers of Jupiter's atmosphere. These scars were the size of Earth and could be seen on Jupiter's surface for many months.

What Killed the Dinosaurs?

One of the great mysteries about the dinosaurs is why they died out so suddenly. Most scientists think that the dinosaurs died when a large comet or asteroid crashed into Earth about 65 million years ago. They believe that the object was about 6 miles (10 kilometers) wide and was traveling a hundred times faster than a bullet when it crashed close to Mexico.

The crash caused a huge explosion, and it sent huge amounts of dust into the atmosphere. The dust blocked out the light of the Sun for many months. Earth got cooler, the dust poisoned the rain, there were lots of fires, and the plants died. The dinosaurs became **extinct** around this time because they could not survive all these changes to the planet.

What Are Asteroids and Where Do They Come From?

Asteroids are lumps of rock that were left over after the Sun and **planets** were made about 4.5 billion years ago. There may be over 10,000 asteroids larger than 60 miles (100 kilometers) across in the **solar system** and many millions of smaller ones. Although asteroids are mainly made of rocks, dust, and water ice, they also contain metals such as iron and nickel.

The main belt

Most of these ancient rocks **orbit** the Sun between the planets Mars and Jupiter. This is the home of about 1 billion asteroids. This region is called the **Asteroid Belt**. The largest asteroid in this belt is Ceres. It is 590 miles (950 kilometers) across, which is almost a quarter of the size of Earth's Moon. Most of the rest of the objects in the Asteroid Belt are about a half a mile (a little less than 1 kilometer) across.

Jupiter is the largest planet in the solar system. **Astronomers** think that the strong pull of its **gravity** stopped all the asteroids in the Asteroid Belt from gathering together to make another planet.

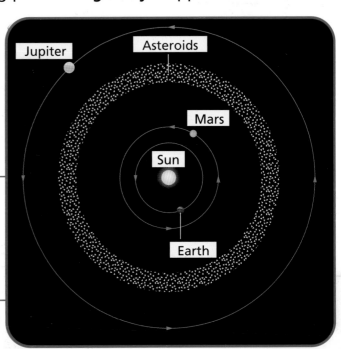

Most of the asteroids in our solar system are in a belt between the orbits of Mars and Jupiter.

Getting really close to asteroids

Most asteroids are too small for us to learn much about them from Earth, even with very large telescopes. Over the past few years, we have discovered more about asteroids by sending **spacecraft** to visit them.

While on its journey to the giant planet Jupiter, the *Galileo* spacecraft gave us our first close-up view of an asteroid. Between 1991 and 1993, it flew past the asteroids Gaspra and Ida. In 1997, the NEAR (Near Earth Asteroid Rendezvous) *Shoemaker* spacecraft passed close to an odd-shaped asteroid called Mathilde. *Shoemaker* then went on to become the first spacecraft to ever go into orbit around an asteroid, when it circled Eros in 2000. A year later it actually landed on Eros, but the spacecraft stopped working soon after.

The Galileo *spacecraft took this picture of asteroid Ida and its tiny moon Dactyl.*

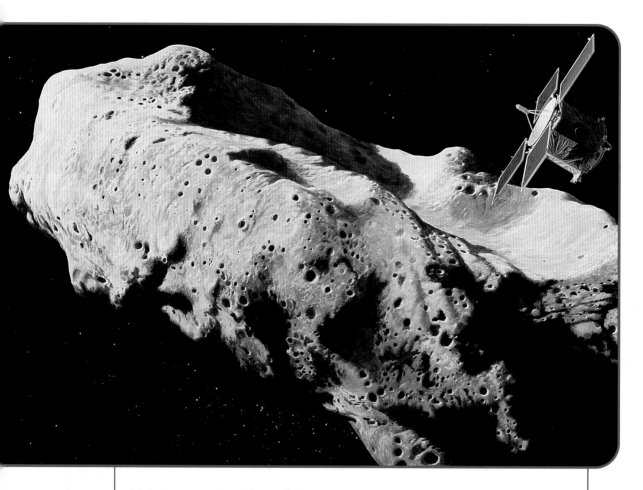

This is an artist's idea of the NEAR (Near Earth Asteroid Rendezvous) **spacecraft** *orbiting the asteroid Eros.*

Asteroids are not solid

The excellent pictures sent back by spacecraft like *Galileo* and *NEAR* showed us that asteroids are rocky objects with lots of **craters** on their surfaces. Amazingly, they also found that many asteroids are not solid. They seem to be made of many pieces. They are more like loosely glued collections of rocks and pebbles.

Another surprise was that the craters on some asteroids are very large. Mathilde is only 40 miles (66 kilometers) long, but it has a crater that is almost 18 miles (30 kilometers) wide and 3.7 miles (6 kilometers) deep. A smaller asteroid crashing into Mathilde caused this crater.

This was one of the last pictures sent by the NEAR spacecraft, when it was three quarters of a mile (1.2 kilometers) above the surface of Eros.

Could I Visit an Asteroid?

You could land on an asteroid, but there would be no air to breathe and no water to drink. The surface would be hilly, with lots of craters and ditches. It would take you less than an hour to walk all around a typical asteroid in the **Asteroid Belt.** Since most asteroids are so small, their **gravity** is very weak. This means you would feel very lightweight standing on the surface. On Eros, a normal adult would weigh as little as a couple of spoonfuls of sugar.

Why Do We Need to Study Asteroids?

Most asteroids are safely tucked away in the **Asteroid Belt** between Mars and Jupiter. However, some have strayed out of this region and have ended up much closer to Earth.

A stray asteroid's **orbit** around the Sun can bring it so close to us that there is a chance it might crash into our **planet.** In 1908, an asteroid, or perhaps a comet, was very close. It exploded in Earth's atmosphere. An area of thick forest almost 25 miles (40 kilometers) across in Siberia, Russia, was destroyed. No one was hurt or killed.

A huge area of forest was destroyed in Russia when an asteroid exploded there in 1908.

If an asteroid the size of a football stadium smashed into one of Earth's oceans, it would make huge waves that could destroy cities along the coasts. A crash from a 6-mile (10-kilometer) wide asteroid or comet would be a danger to almost all life on our planet.

This is an artist's idea of a giant asteroid smashing into Earth. If this happened today, it could destroy all life on our planet.

No need to panic

There is no need to panic. The chances of an asteroid actually hitting Earth are very small. No asteroid or comet is known to be heading toward us today, but we do need to keep watching. There are more than 100,000 asteroids, each the size of a football stadium, that could pass close to Earth. All around the world **astronomers** use telescopes to watch these asteroids. This way they can work out if any of them might be a danger to us.

What could be done?

In the very unlikely event that scientists discover an asteroid in space heading toward Earth, it is hoped that we will know about it many years before it gets close. There would then be enough time to launch rockets toward the asteroid and set off huge explosions above its surface. The force of the explosions would change the asteroid's orbit slightly, so that it would not hit Earth.

What's the Difference Between Meteors and Meteorites?

The **solar system** is littered with lots of small rocks and bits of dust. As Earth moves in its **orbit** around the Sun, these objects may enter Earth's **atmosphere.** They will heat up when they rub against the planet's atmosphere. This heating up is caused by **friction.**

The smaller objects from space heat up and melt completely in the atmosphere. They leave behind the streaks of light in the sky called meteors. Anything between the size of dust grains and the size of ping-pong balls will be too small to survive the journey through the atmosphere to Earth's surface. They will end their lives as meteors.

*Some scientists think this **meteorite,** found in Antarctica in 1984, was blasted from the surface of Mars about 3.5 billion years ago.*

Chunks that land

Some chunks of material approaching our **planet** from space are large enough to survive the scorching trip through Earth's atmosphere. Pieces that land on our planet's surface are called meteorites. They are usually just a few inches across when they land.

Thousands of meteorites hit Earth every day. Nearly all of them land in the oceans or in places with very few people.

These scientists are collecting meteorites on the icy surface of Antarctica.

Finding meteorites is important because they are very old objects. This means that scientists can use them to learn more about the solar system when it was first made, billions of years ago. Most meteorites are pieces of comets or asteroids. Amazingly, some meteorites have even been blasted from Mars or the Moon and have crashed on to Earth. Antarctica, near Earth's **South Pole,** is a good place for finding meteorites. They are dark and easy to spot against the bright white ice.

Most meteorites are made of stone or rock. A few are made of metals like iron, and a tiny number are a mixture of stone and iron.

What Are Meteor Showers?

If you look at a dark, starry sky, you will sometimes see streaks or flashes of light. These are meteors and you can usually see two or three of them every hour, every night.

Free fireworks displays

During some months of the year, many more meteors than normal can be seen at night. Perhaps as many as 100 meteors per hour may streak across the skies, looking like a fireworks display. These events are **meteor showers.** One of the greatest meteor showers ever seen was on November 12, 1833. People living in Europe and the United States saw almost 100 meteors every second.

Burning comet dust

Comets that pass close to Earth leave behind huge clouds of tiny dust grains. The material is spread out in space, all through the **orbit** of the comet.

This Perseid meteor trail was photographed in Finland. The Perseid meteor showers are usually seen around August 12 each year.

Meteor showers happen when Earth passes through these clouds of leftover comet dust. At this time, lots of dust grains crash into Earth's **atmosphere** and flash across the sky as bright streaks of light.

A meteor shower ends when Earth has completely passed through the dust cloud. We then have to wait a few months for the next meteor shower, when Earth comes across the dust of another comet.

Showers to Watch For

Most meteor showers seem to start from single points in the sky and streak out like exploding fireworks. The showers are named after the **constellation** of stars from which they seem to come. The best place to watch these displays is somewhere far away from city lights.

The best meteor showers in the **Northern Hemisphere** are the Quadrantid shower in early January, the Perseid shower in mid-August, the Leonid shower in mid-November, and the Geminid shower in mid-December. These showers can be seen each year. The Perseid, Leonid, and Geminid showers can also be seen from Australia and other countries in the **Southern Hemisphere.**

These meteors are part of the Leonid shower of 1999.

27

Fact File

Here are some interesting facts about comets, asteroids, and meteors:

- The dust grains that cause the Perseid **meteor shower** every August were left behind by a comet that passed close to Earth in 1862. The dust grains that cause the Leonid meteor shower every November were left behind by a comet called Tempel-Tuttle.

- The **Asteroid Belt**, where most asteroids are found, is about three times farther away from the Sun than Earth.

- For two centuries the largest known asteroid was Ceres, which is 590 miles (950 kilometers) across. In 2001, an icy rock called 2001 KX76 was found beyond Pluto. It is 745 miles (1,200 kilometers) across, which is almost half the size of Pluto, the smallest planet. If proven to be a true asteroid, it will hold the record as the largest known asteroid in the **solar system.**

- Comets near Earth move through space at a speed of about 60,000 miles per hour (100,000 kilometers per hour).

A bright, glowing comet can be one of the most fantastic sights of nature.

This is an artist's idea of what the Rosetta Lander probe would look like on the surface of Comet Wirtanen.

- **Meteoroids** enter Earth's **atmosphere** at different speeds, depending on their size. Those larger than about 100 feet (30 meters) can be traveling at about 60,000 miles per hour (100,000 kilometers per hour). After being slowed by the **friction** of the atmosphere, a **meteorite** may still be moving at 3,000 miles per hour (5,000 kilometers per hour) when it hits the ground.

- In 2003, the European Space Agency will launch the *Rosetta* **spacecraft** toward a comet called Wirtanen. It will land on the comet in 2013 to study its surface.

Glossary

Asteroid Belt doughnut-shaped collection of asteroids found between the **orbits** of Mars and Jupiter

astronomer scientist who studies objects in space, such as **planets** and stars

atmosphere layers of gases that surround a planet

carbon dioxide gas contained in Earth's air

coma large cloud of gas that surrounds the **nucleus** of a comet as it gets close to the Sun

constellation imaginary pattern or picture formed in the sky by a group of stars

crater bowl-shaped hole made on the surface of a **planet** or moon by the crash of a rocky object from space

dust tail part of a comet's tail made up of tiny dust grains

extinct no longer living

friction force between two objects when they rub against each other

gas tail part of a comet's tail that is made up of gas

gravity force that pulls all objects toward the surface of Earth or any other **planet,** moon, or star

Kuiper belt region beyond Pluto that scientists think contains large numbers of comets

meteoroid rock or dust that travels through space

meteorite rock or dust that enters Earth's atmosphere from space and hits Earth's surface

meteor shower event during certain times of the year when many meteors can be seen every hour

microscopic something extremely tiny that can only be seen using a microscope

Northern Hemisphere the half of Earth between the **North Pole** and the equator

nucleus center of an object,

Oort cloud huge group of rocks and dust that surround the **solar system**

orbit path taken by an object as it moves around another object (planet or star)

particle very small piece, or amount, of an object or material

planet large object (for example, Earth) moving around a star (for example, the Sun)

solar system group of nine **planets** and other objects **moving around** the Sun

solar wind steady stream of material given off by the Sun

Southern Hemisphere the half of Earth between the **South Pole** and the equator

South Pole point due south that marks the end of an imaginary line, called an axis, about which a **planet** spins

spacecraft human-made vehicle that travels beyond Earth and into space

More Books to Read

Bortz, Fred. *Collision Course: Cosmic Impacts and Life on Earth.* Brookfield, Conn.: Millbrook Press, 2001.

Cefrey, Holly. *What if an Asteroid Hit Earth?* Danbury, Conn.: Children's Press, 2002.

Sipiera, Paul P. *Comets and Meteor Showers.* Danbury, Conn.: Children's Press, 1997.

Index